Research Report
October 2009

CONSORTIUM ON CHICAGO SCHOOL RESEARCH AT THE UNIVERSITY OF CHICAGO

When Schools Close
Effects on Displaced Students in Chicago Public Schools

Marisa de la Torre and Julia Gwynne

Acknowledgements

We would like to acknowledge the many people who helped make this report possible. Our colleagues at the Consortium on Chicago School Research at the University of Chicago Urban Education Institute gave critical feedback at each stage of this project. In particular, Marshall Jean helped us with preliminary analyses. In addition, Elaine Allensworth, Penny Bender Sebring, Melissa Roderick, Sue Sporte, Chris Mazzeo, and Diane Rado each provided us with thoughtful comments on this manuscript. We are also indebted to members of the Steering Committee and others who gave us very useful comments on this work. Donald Fraynd, Josie Yanguas, and Arie van der Ploeg performed careful reviews of this manuscript. Claire Durwood was instrumental in helping us edit and produce this report. We also thank Amy Proger who provided a thorough technical read of the final report.

We have also benefited from discussions with Chicago Public Schools (CPS) senior staff. Our work would not have been possible without the student record data archive provided by CPS. In particular, we thank the CPS staff at the Office of Research, Evaluation, and Accountability for their efforts.

This study was made possible by a grant from the John D. and Catherine T. MacArthur Foundation.

Table of Contents

Executive Summary 1

Introduction.. 5

Chapter 1: *School Closing Policy in Chicago*................................... 9

Chapter 2: *Where Do Displaced Students Go? A Look at Receiving Schools* 13

Chapter 3: *What Are the Effects on Displaced Students?* 17

Chapter 4: *Interpretative Summary*..25

References 27

Appendix A: *School Closings and New Openings*.........................29

Appendix B: *Data, Analytic Methods, and Variables Used* 32

Endnotes 39

Executive Summary

Few decisions by a school district are more controversial than the decision to close a school. School staff, students and their families, and even the local community all bear a substantial burden once the decision is made to close a school. Teachers and other school staff must search for new employment, students are faced with a multitude of adjustments that come from enrolling in new schools, and neighborhoods lose a central institution in their community.

While recognizing these challenges, Chicago Public Schools (CPS) has insisted on the need to close schools for two reasons. First, CPS has stressed the educational necessity of closing schools that demonstrate chronically low levels of academic performance. They argue that, despite the difficulties associated with changing schools, students in failing schools would be better served by transferring into schools that are academically more successful.[1] Second, CPS has also emphasized the financial necessity of closing schools with student enrollments far below their intended capacity.[2]

Since 2001, CPS has closed 44 schools for reasons of poor academic performance or underutilization. In 2006, CPS modified its school closing policy to focus on "turning around" academically weak schools instead of closing them. In a turnaround school, students are allowed to remain in the same building while all or most of the staff is replaced. As of 2009, there are 12 turnaround schools in Chicago.

Despite the attention that school closings have received in the past few years, very little is known about how displaced students fare after their schools are closed. This report examines the impact that closing schools had on the students who attended these schools. We focus on regular elementary schools that were closed between 2001 and 2006 for underutilization or low performance and ask whether students who were forced to leave these schools

> The learning outcomes of displaced students depend on the characteristics of receiving schools.

and enroll elsewhere experienced any positive or negative effects from this type of school move.[3] We look at a number of student outcomes, including reading and math achievement, special education referrals, retentions, summer school attendance, mobility, and high school performance. We also examine characteristics of the receiving schools and ask whether differences in these schools had any impact on the learning experiences of the students who transferred into them.

In order to assess the effects that school closings had on students, we compare students ages eight and older who were displaced by school closings to a group of students in similar schools that did not close. This comparison group of students allows us to estimate how the displaced students would have performed on a range of outcomes had their schools not been closed. We report six major findings:

1. **Most students who transferred out of closing schools reenrolled in schools that were academically weak.**

   Although some of the receiving schools had higher achievement levels than the schools that were closed, a large number of displaced students reenrolled in some of the weakest schools in the system. For example, 40 percent of displaced students enrolled in schools on probation and 42 percent of displaced students enrolled in receiving schools where the scores on the Iowa Tests of Basic Skills (ITBS) were in the lowest quartile of the distribution of scores in the system. Only 6 percent of displaced students attended schools with ITBS scores in the top quartile. Most of the students who enrolled in receiving schools with strong academic environments did not attend the school in their designated attendance area and traveled an average of 3.5 miles from their home neighborhood to attend school.

2. **The largest negative impact of school closings on students' reading and math achievement occurred in the year before the schools were closed.**

   Announcements about upcoming CPS school closings typically were made in January—about six months prior to the actual closings of schools and a few months before students took annual achievement tests. These announcements often caused significant angst for students, parents, teachers, and other community members, and the disruption may have hindered student learning. Students' reading scores on the ITBS showed a loss of about one-and-a-half months of learning during the announcement year. In math, the loss of learning was equivalent to a little more than half a month.

3. **Once students left schools slated for closing, on average the additional effects on their learning were neither negative nor positive.**

   One year after students left their closed schools, their achievement in reading and math was not significantly different from what we would have expected had their schools not been closed. During this time, students overcame the negative impact suffered during the announcement year and returned to their expected learning trajectory. Achievement remained at this expected level two and three years after their schools were closed.

4. **Although the school closing policy had only a small overall effect on student test scores, it did affect summer school enrollment and subsequent school mobility.**

   Students who left closing schools were less likely to enroll in Summer Bridge the summer after their schools closed.[4] Most of the schools that were slated for closing shut down immediately after the end of the academic year, leaving the receiving schools with the task of providing summer school for displaced students in third, sixth, and eighth grade. However, a number of receiving schools reported waiting several months before obtaining academic records for incoming displaced students. In addition, displaced students were more likely to change schools a second time after their initial displacement, either during the academic year or during the summer.

5. **When displaced students reached high school, their on-track rates to graduate were no different than the rates of students who attended schools similar to those that closed.**

   Students whose schools closed at the end of their eighth-grade year entered high school with reading and math scores below their expected level as a result of the disruption caused by the announcements of upcoming closures. Students who were in earlier grades when their schools closed entered high school with reading achievement at the expected level. The impact of school closings was not large enough to affect the on-track rates for displaced students once they reached high school, regardless of their age at the closing.

6. **The learning outcomes of displaced students depended on the characteristics of receiving schools.**
Displaced students who enrolled in new schools with high average achievement had larger gains in both reading and math than students who enrolled in receiving schools with lower average achievement. Furthermore, displaced students who enrolled in schools with high levels of student-teacher trust and teacher personal attention also had larger gains in both reading and math, compared to students in receiving schools with low levels of teacher support.[5]

Overall, we found few effects, either positive or negative, of school closings on the achievement of displaced students. The lack of a more substantial positive effect of transferring students out of these schools is likely due to the types of receiving schools that students transferred into. Displaced students who enrolled in receiving schools with strong academic quality or with high levels of teacher support had higher learning gains than displaced students who enrolled in other receiving schools. However, the number of displaced students who attended these strong schools was small. Only 6 percent of displaced students enrolled in academically strong schools, while 42 percent of displaced students continued to attend schools with very low levels of academic achievement.

Introduction

Closing schools is one of the most controversial decisions a school district can make. Between 2001 and 2006, Chicago Public Schools (CPS) closed 38 schools. Most of the schools were closed either for low enrollment relative to the school's capacity (17 schools) or for chronic underperformance (9 schools). The central argument behind closing underutilized schools is that schools functioning below capacity are more expensive to run compared to other schools. In addition, providing proper services for students is harder in schools operating below capacity. Savings from closing underutilized schools can be allocated towards other areas, particularly given the fiscal challenges CPS is facing and the state of the current economy.[6] The main argument in favor of closing low performing schools is that doing so provides an opportunity for students to attend higher performing schools with stronger learning environments.

Not surprisingly, the efforts of CPS and other districts to close schools have led to significant controversy in Chicago and many other cities nationwide. Critics of school closings stress the disruption that school closings create for students who attend those schools and for the schools that receive a large number of displaced students. Research has shown that student mobility is associated with lower subsequent achievement, higher retention rates, higher number of referrals to special education, and a much lower likelihood of graduating.[7] Critics of school closings also emphasize the disruption that moving to a new school causes in terms of social capital formation. Ties to adults and other students are severed, and new ties need to be formed in the new school.[8] Other criticisms focus on the potential impact that an influx of new students will have on different aspects of school life in receiving schools.[9] Accommodating a large number of new students could create tension and stress for the staff, especially if these schools lack resources to integrate displaced students.[10]

> Between 2001 and 2006, CPS closed 17 schools for underutilization and nine for underperformance.

Recently, CPS's school closing policy has come under fire in both the local and national media. Newspaper articles have quoted activists who blame school closings, and the subsequent shuffling of students across rival gang lines, for a surge in teen violence.

Advocates for closings argue that any potential disruption created by a school move is more than offset by increased learning in higher quality schools. And in fact, other researchers have found that students who change schools in pursuit of higher academic quality do tend to benefit from the move.[11]

Despite the debate that surrounds Chicago's school closing policy, very little is known about the effect of closing schools. This report specifically examines the impact of closing schools on the students who attended these schools and considers four main questions:

1. Where do students go after their schools close? How different are the receiving schools from the closing schools?

2. Do displaced students suffer any kind of disruption in learning due to the closing of their schools? If so, when does it start and how long does it last?

3. Do school closings improve the educational prospects of displaced students?

4. Do characteristics of receiving schools shape the educational prospects of displaced students? If so, what are those school characteristics and how much do they help students?

To answer these questions, we focus on a group of regular elementary schools that were closed between 2001 and 2006 for either low enrollment or low performance (see Chapter 2 for an explanation of how we selected the group of schools for this study). Our sample contains 18 schools with 5,445 students who were enrolled in kindergarten through eighth grade just prior to the closing. With the exception of the first question, our subsequent analyses focus on students who were eight years and older attending these schools and compare them to students of the same age who attended schools similar to those that closed.

The focus of this study is on the academic effects of school closings on students who were forced to change schools. The study does not address the social or emotional aspects of school closings; nor does it consider the issue of student violence. It is not an evaluation of the full impact of the school closing policy. A comprehensive evaluation of school closings would have to include an evaluation of the effects on the receiving schools and on the future cohorts of students who would have attended the closing schools, as well as the effects on the displaced students.

The Debate around Transforming the Lowest Performing Schools

In recent months, the idea of "turning around" the lowest performing schools has become prominent in the national debate on education reform. Turnarounds have been actively promoted by Arne Duncan, U.S. Secretary of Education and former Chicago Public Schools CEO, and others as a necessary step for the most troubled schools in the nation. Many of the supporters of turnarounds highlight the experiences of CPS schools that have gone through a similar process. Dodge Elementary School, which was closed in 2002 and reopened in the fall of 2003, has been mentioned as an example of a successful CPS turnaround.

Amidst all the national attention to turnarounds, few have noted that CPS has actually implemented two distinct models of transforming the lowest performing schools. From 2001 to 2006, the period covered in this report, CPS employed a "school closing" strategy that resulted in some underperforming schools being closed permanently; others, like Dodge, were closed temporarily and then "re-started" a year later. More recently, CPS has employed what it calls a "turnaround" approach, in which schools remain open but all or most of the adults in the building are dismissed and new staff is hired. When schools are closed, students are displaced and, in cases like Dodge, they have the option of coming back to the newly reopened school. In turnarounds, however, students are not forced to change schools.

While displaced students such as those from Dodge are part of our study, this study does not examine the effects either of "re-starting" in chronically low performing schools or of the turnaround strategy.

Chapter 1

School Closing Policy in Chicago

The CPS policy on closing schools states that a school can be closed for three reasons: non-academic reasons, academic reasons, and a need for change in educational focus.[12] Non-academic reasons include underutilization of a school's space, poor physical condition of the building, the need for an alternative use of the school's facilities, or the conversion of the school to a charter school. Academic reasons include a school's failure to improve its academic performance after being placed on probation. School closings due to a change in educational focus address the possibility of implementing a new curriculum or instructional programs that will result in dramatic changes in faculty or students.

Most of the school closings in CPS have fallen into the categories of low capacity utilization of the school building and academic reasons (see Table 1). The vast majority of closed schools in these two categories have been elementary schools. Between 2001 and 2006, CPS closed 13 regular elementary schools for underutilization and nine for academic reasons. A relatively small number of schools have been closed for each of the other reasons.

> In 2007, 147 schools had enrollments below 50 percent of their capacity.

TABLE 1

Number and reasons for school closings between 2001 and 2006

Non-Academic Reasons	Number of Schools
• Underutilization	13 Elementary Schools, 4 Alternative Schools
• Condition of the Building	1 Elementary School, 2 High Schools
• Alternative Use of School	1 Elementary School, 2 High Schools
• Conversion to Charter School	None
Academic Reasons	9 Elementary Schools
Change in Educational Focus	3 High Schools
Other	1 Elementary School
Unknown Reasons	1 Elementary School, 1 Alternative School

Do New Schools Open in Buildings that Are Vacated by Closed Schools?

The answer is yes in many cases, but not always. With the introduction in 2004 of the Renaissance 2010 initiative, which establishes that more than 100 high quality schools will be opened by the year 2010, many buildings that housed schools that were closed are now used for new schools. Appendix A provides a list of the new schools that opened in buildings vacated by closed schools, the year that new schools were opened, and the grade structure offered in the new schools. For example, Williams closed at the end of the 2001–02 school year, and four new schools opened in the same building in the 2003–04 school year. Fourteen buildings that housed schools that were closed have never been used by new schools.

Some displaced students chose to enroll in new schools that opened in buildings where their old schools had been. But in some cases, new schools did not serve the same grades as old schools. As a result, some displaced students who lived in close proximity to these new schools could not enroll in them. Also, many of the new schools were charter or contract schools, rather than neighborhood schools. Because charter schools and contract schools do not have traditional attendance area boundaries, students had to submit an application in order to enroll; this may have been a barrier for some displaced students to enroll in these schools.

In general, CPS enrollment has been declining over the last few years, reflecting recent population trends that have led to a decrease in the number of school-aged children in the city of Chicago.[13] However, most of the schools that were closed for low enrollment in the mid-2000s were schools in close proximity to public housing. As the number of buildings demolished by the Chicago Housing Authority (CHA) increased, more and more nearby schools experienced substantial decreases in their enrollment.[14]

CPS defines underutilized schools as those with an enrollment that is below 65 percent of their capacity, and a large number of CPS schools fall into this category.[15] Schools that were closed for this reason had enrollment capacities well below this number; in most cases, a large proportion of their students were living outside the attendance area.[16] In 2007, 147 schools had enrollments below 50 percent of their capacity.[17] CPS closed eight of these schools at the end of the 2009 academic year, and four more will be phased out grade-by-grade over time.[18]

According to CPS policy, chronically low performing schools are those that have been on probation for at least one year and have failed to make progress. To measure progress and to decide whether to close schools for academic reasons, CPS uses such indicators as probation status history, test scores, and annual students' gains over time. However, each year many more schools meet the criteria for being closed than are actually selected. In the past, CPS was criticized for the lack of transparency that surrounded the decision to close certain schools.[19] In an effort to be more systematic and transparent in the decision-making process, CPS amended the school closing policy in 2007 so that schools with new principals, schools that had previously been designated as receiving schools for other closed schools, and schools that had no higher performing schools in close proximity would not be considered for closing. All schools closed for academic reasons were on probation and had less than a quarter of their students at or above norms on the reading portion of the ITBS or meeting or exceeding state standards on the Illinois Standards Achievement Test (ISAT).

In most cases, schools that were in close proximity to closing schools had their attendance area boundaries redrawn to accommodate displaced students. The policy also specified that displaced students could apply to any school, subject to space availability, as is always the case with the CPS open enrollment policy.[20] The policy also emphasized that students who are displaced for academic reasons should be reassigned to higher performing schools with available spaces.

Over time, the public has grown more discontented with the closing of schools.[21] Teachers, parents, and other community members have become increasingly unhappy with the rapid increase in the number of school closings, the limited input that the public has had in the process, and the fact that displaced students typically do not enroll in schools that perform better than the ones they left behind. In addition, receiving schools have struggled to accommodate an influx of new students, sometimes more than once, with few extra resources provided to integrate them.[22] CPS has responded to the public by limiting the closing of schools for academic reasons, focusing instead on creating turnaround schools in which students are allowed to remain in the same building after almost all of the school staff is replaced. As of 2009, there are 12 turnaround schools in Chicago.

Chapter 2

Where Do Displaced Students Go? A Look at Receiving Schools

Receiving schools play a central role in the debate on school closings. A frequently voiced criticism is that receiving schools did not look dramatically different from schools that were closed.[23] If students were to benefit from the move, receiving schools should be of higher academic quality than the schools left by displaced students.[24] In the last section we described how schools became designated receiving schools, but at the same time the school closing policy established that students could apply to any other school in the system with available seats. CPS encouraged students to enroll in high performing schools, especially if they were displaced because of academic reasons.

In this chapter, we explore which schools were the designated receiving schools, where displaced students actually went after the closings, and how the actual receiving schools ranked on a series of indicators. Our study focuses on 18 schools; nine closed for underutilization and nine for academic reasons between 2001 and 2006.[25] We focus on the 5,445 students who were enrolled in May just before closing, and we describe the elementary schools they attended the next September.[26]

Table 2 contains a list of the closing schools with information on the year of closing, the reason for closing, the percent capacity utilization, the percent of students at or above norms on the ITBS reading test in the year prior to closing, and a list of the designated receiving schools. Table 2 shows that schools closed for underutilization had very low levels of capacity utilization, but they also had low levels of achievement. Conversely, schools

> A large proportion of displaced students enrolled in schools with weak academic performance.

closed for underperformance had very low achievement levels, but they also had low capacity utilization. Even though schools were closed for one particular reason, these two groups of schools were very similar in both capacity utilization and achievement levels.

The last column in Table 2 shows the designated receiving schools for each closing school. Table 2 also includes the percent of students in receiving and closing schools who scored at or above national norms on the ITBS. On average, schools that were designated as receiving schools showed achievement levels that were somewhat higher than the closing school, but, in most instances, the differences were not large. In fact, some of the designated receiving schools were later closed for academic reasons. Other designated receiving schools were closed later because of underutilization.[28] This reflects the fact that surrounding schools in neighborhoods that were experiencing depopulation also had low enrollment numbers and were subsequently closed because of underutilization.

Most of the displaced students reenrolled in a traditional neighborhood CPS school, but not necessarily in the receiving school that was designated for them. Of the students who were displaced, 96 percent attended other CPS schools, with the rest leaving for private schools in the city or moving outside the city. Of the

TABLE 2
Closed schools and the designated receiving schools

Last Year in Operation	School Name	Reason for Closing	% Capacity Utilization[27]	% Students at/above Norms ITBS Reading	Designated Receiving Schools (% Students at/above Norms ITBS Reading)
2000–01	Riis	Underutilization	50.6	25.2	Jefferson (15.7) and W. Brown (20.0)
2001–02	Dodge	Academic Reasons	30.2	14.1	Calhoun North (21.2), Cather (27.4), Dett (31.2), and Grant (21.4)
2001–02	Williams	Academic Reasons	49.5	12.9	Douglas (32.8), Drake (33.1), and Ward (38.1)
2001–02	Terrell	Academic Reasons	19.8	13.0	Beethoven (42.4), Coleman (28.5), and Farren (22.6)
2002–03	Colman	Underutilization	18.7	37.1	Beethoven (49.0)
2002–03	Donoghue	Underutilization	18.0	28.9	Doolittle West and Doolittle East (23.4)
2003–04	Byrd	Underutilization	39.4	17.8	Jenner (26.7)
2003–04	Douglas	Underutilization	34.7	29.5	Drake (39.6) and Mayo (46.8)
2003–04	Hartigan	Underutilization	29.2	15.4	Attucks (31.9)
2003–04	Jefferson	Underutilization	41.1	17.1	Smyth (23.1) and Gladstone (28.4)
2003–04	Raymond	Underutilization	19.2	27.3	Attucks (31.9)
2003–04	Suder	Underutilization	27.4	25.4	Herbert (33.5) and W. Brown (28.4)
2004–05	Grant	Academic Reasons	19.3	16.2	Herbert (34.7) and Calhoun North (21.8)
2004–05	Howland	Academic Reasons	31.7	18.6	Dvorak (42.3), Johnson (35.3), and Pope (37.6)
2004–05	Bunche	Academic Reasons	49.4	21.0	Earle (27.3), O'Toole (35.3), and Goodlow (25.9)
2005–06	Farren	Academic Reasons	15.4	14.8	Beethoven (48.0)
2005–06	Morse	Academic Reasons	58.9	17.5	Morton (20.4), Ryerson (31.9), and Lafayette (43.2)
2005–06	Frazier	Academic Reasons	39.5	23.1	Gregory (34.1), Sumner (36.3), Webster (35.0), and Henson (22.6)

displaced students who reenrolled in CPS elementary schools, 97 percent attended a neighborhood school but less than half attended one of the designated receiving schools. Because many students attending closing schools were not living in their school's attendance area, it is possible that some chose to attend schools closer to their residences.

Other CPS schools that were not designated as receiving schools also enrolled displaced students. A handful of these schools enrolled a large number of students, while many others enrolled just a few. Table 3 shows the number of students who enrolled each year in designated and non-designated receiving schools. For example, of the 261 students who had to transfer to new schools when Riis closed in 2001, 112 enrolled in Jefferson, which was a designated receiving school. None of the students enrolled in Brown, which was also a designated school; however, 49 enrolled in Smyth, which was not a designated school. The remaining 100 students enrolled in 40 other CPS schools.

Characteristics of Receiving Schools

A large proportion of displaced students enrolled in schools with weak academic performance. Almost 40 percent of displaced students enrolled in receiving

TABLE 3

Designated and actual receiving schools

Last Year in Operation	School Name (Number of Students Reenrolling in Elementary Grades)	Designated Receiving Schools (Number of Displaced Students Enrolling in School)	Other Schools Receiving 30 or More Students (Number of Displaced Students Enrolling in School)	Total Number of Receiving Schools
2000–01	Riis (261)	Jefferson (112) and W. Brown (0)	Smyth (49)	40
2001–02	Dodge Williams Terrell (1,071)	Douglas (161), Drake (113), Farren (54), Cather (44), Grant (35), Calhoun North (30), Dett (30), Beethoven (14), Ward (1), and Coleman (0)	National Teachers Academy (326)	117
2002–03	Colman Donoghue (260)	Beethoven (65), Doolittle East (40), and Doolittle West (39)		44
2003–04	Byrd Douglas Hartigan Jefferson Raymond Suder (1,457)	Attucks (146), Jenner (145), Smyth (89), Drake (82), Gladstone (79), Mayo (63), Hebert (52), and W. Brown (27)	Dett (50), Doolittle (42), and Medill (33)	192
2004–05	Grant Howland Bunche (841)	O'Toole (75), Johnson (70), Herbert (46), Calhoun North (38), Pope (34), Earle (33), Dvorak (28), and Goodlow (11)		163
2005–06	Farren Morse Frazier (798)	Morton (153), Henson (111), Beethoven (58), Sumner (43), Ryerson (36), Gregory (13), Webster (9), and Lafayette (5)		141

schools that were on academic probation. Forty-two percent of displaced students enrolled in receiving schools with ITBS scores that were in the lowest quartile of the elementary schools in the system, 38 percent in the second quartile, 13 percent in the third quartile, and 6 percent in the top quartile.

Students who enrolled in schools in the top quartile entered schools with very different environments than those they left. These schools had better attendance rates and higher student stability than the closed schools: the attendance rate averaged 95.5 percent; on average, 94.7 percent of the students in these schools remained in the schools during the academic year. Furthermore, none of these schools were on probation. By contrast, at receiving schools in the lowest quartile, the attendance rate was 91.1 percent; the stability rate, on average, was 86.9 percent; and 72 percent of displaced students entered schools that were on probation.

Most of the students who enrolled in schools with strong academic environments traveled longer distances from home than other students because these schools were often outside the attendance areas of the displaced students.[29] As we described in the previous section, designated receiving schools were in close proximity to the closing schools. While families of displaced students were informed about the opportunity to apply to other CPS schools with available seats, some families limited the range of schools students could attend to the ones nearby because they objected to sending their children across town. Of the students who enrolled in very low performing receiving schools (schools in the bottom quartile), 73 percent were enrolled in their attendance area schools; these students traveled an average of half a mile to school. Only 17 percent of the students who enrolled in top performing schools (in the top quartile) attended schools in their attendance area. Most students who enrolled in top performing schools traveled an average of 3.5 miles to school.

The fact that very few displaced students enrolled in top performing CPS schools could have been the result of few seats being available in those schools; or, because these schools were far from students' residences, parents might not have been comfortable sending their children to unfamiliar neighborhoods. Students' test scores were not a barrier to enrolling in these schools. Seventy percent of the displaced students who enrolled in top performing schools had reading scores below norms.

Chapter 3

What Are the Effects on Displaced Students?

In order to estimate the effects of closings on the displaced students, we focus on students who were eight years and older in the 18 elementary schools in our sample. We follow these students and compare them to students of the same age who attended schools that were similar to those that closed (see Appendix B for a description of how we picked schools that were similar to those that closed). We limit our sample to students eight years and older because each year these students were required to take the ITBS test in reading and math. We also use the available history of test scores prior to school closings to estimate the effects on displaced students, given their earlier performance (see Appendix B for a description of the statistical models used in the following analyses).

> School closings had a negative impact on reading and math achievement the year of the announcement (a few months before the school actually closed).

Measuring the Effects on Achievement

To estimate the effects of closing schools on students' achievement, we use test scores of the displaced students before and after their schools closed. We also use test scores of students in the comparison group from the same period. Because the comparison group of students had backgrounds that were very similar to the displaced students and attended schools that were similar to those that closed, we can use their test scores to estimate how displaced students would have performed had their schools not closed. We then compare this "expected learning trajectory" for displaced students to their actual learning trajectory (see Figure A for a depiction of both trajectories). The difference between these two is the estimated effect of school closings.

We report these differences in terms of monthly learning differences. Based on the expected learning trajectory, we can calculate how much the student was expected to learn annually; by dividing that by 10, we can calculate how much they should have learned per month. We divide the difference between the expected achievement and actual achievement by this monthly learning gain to translate our results into differences in learning measured in months.

FIGURE A

Simulated example of expected and actual learning trajectories for displaced students

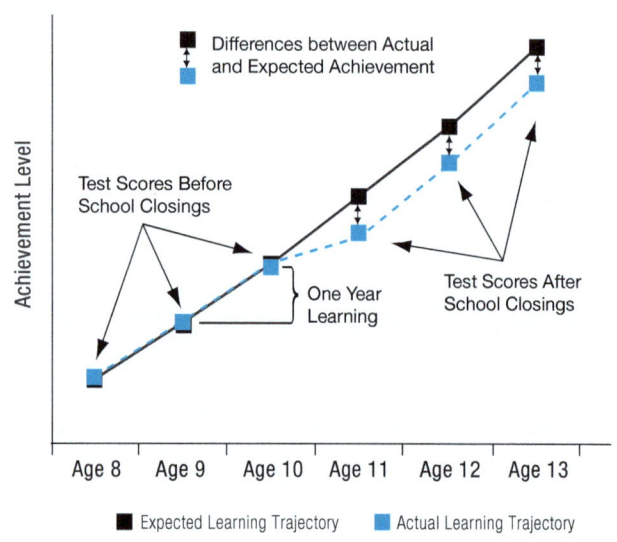

Impact of School Closings on Reading and Math Achievement

School closings had a negative impact on reading and math achievement the year of the announcement (a few months before the school actually closed). Announcements about upcoming CPS school closings were typically made by the Board of Education in January, about six months prior to the actual closing of schools and just a few months before students took the annual achievement tests. During this announcement year, reading achievement for students in schools slated for closing was about one-and-a-half months of learning below the expected level, and math achievement was more than half a month below the expected level. Figure 1 shows the short-term impact that school closings had on the achievement of students who attended these schools.

The lower achievement may have been caused by the disruption that followed announcements of

FIGURE 1

Students' achievement was negatively affected by the announcement of the school closings; one year after closing, students' achievement was no different from the achievement of the comparison group of students

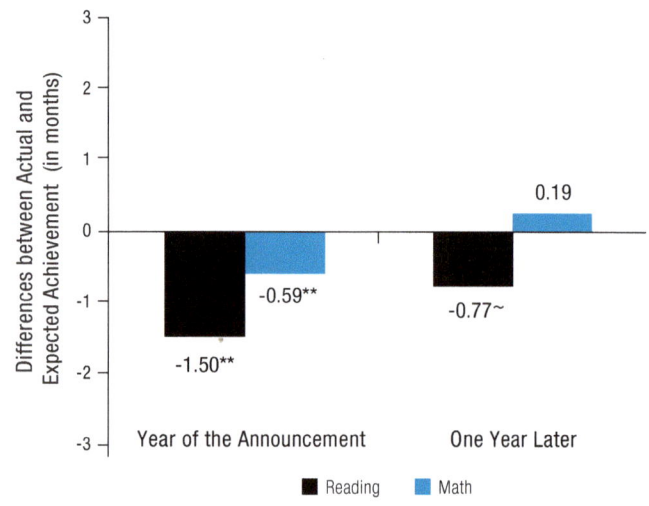

Note: ** p-value < 0.01; * p-value < 0.05; ~ p-value < 0.10

upcoming CPS school closings. After CPS identified schools slated for closing, there were typically protests by school staff, parents, and community leaders. Parents and community leaders were irate that children would be forced to endure the upheaval of relocating to new schools. Teachers were frustrated by the news that they would soon have to find new employment. And, despite recognizing the importance of continuing to educate students, some teachers also reported difficulties staying motivated.[30] These events were likely to impact students, which may explain the drop in learning gains shortly after learning their schools would close.

Once students left schools slated for closing, there were no additional negative effects on achievement. In fact, one year later, displaced students' reading and math achievement had returned to their expected level.[31] Although displaced students were likely to have experienced some difficulties in adjusting to their new schools, on average these challenges had no apparent impact on their learning.

As Figure 2 shows, there were no long-term effects on the math achievement of displaced students.[32] In reading, displaced students were about one-and-a-half months behind in learning two years after their schools closed; however, this difference between their actual learning and their expected learning is not statistically significant.[33] Three years after schools closed, displaced students were about one-and-a-half months ahead of their expected learning in reading; but, again, this difference is not statistically significant.

Impact of School Closings on Other Outcomes

Although school closings had little impact on achievement, they did have an effect on other outcomes. Figure 3 shows the impact of the closing policy on Summer Bridge enrollment for third-, sixth-, and eighth-grade students. During the summer prior to their schools' closing, displaced students were just as likely to attend Summer Bridge as students in the comparison group. However, during the summer after their schools closed, only a quarter of displaced students enrolled in Summer Bridge, compared to 29 percent of students in the comparison group with similar characteristics.

Most of the schools that were slated for closing shut down immediately after the end of the academic year,

FIGURE 2

In the long run students' achievement did not suffer from school closing; neither did it improve upon the expected learning trajectory

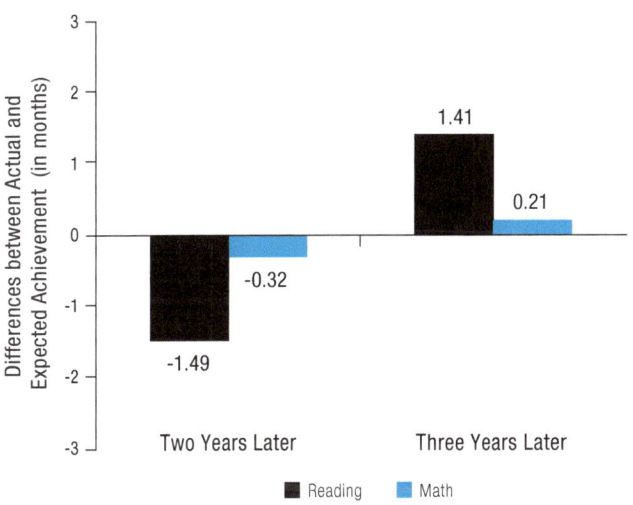

Note: These estimates are based on a reduced sample of students for whom we have data three years after closings take place.

** p-value < 0.01; * p-value < 0.05; ~ p-value < 0.10

FIGURE 3

Displaced students were less likely to attend Summer Bridge immediately after closing

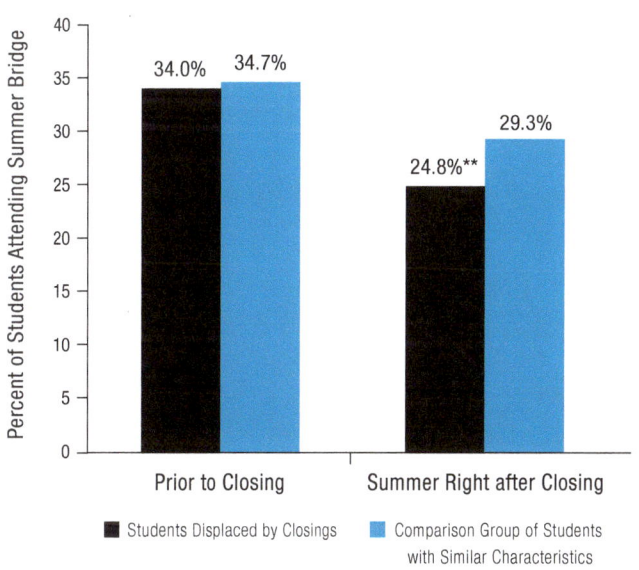

Note: ** p-value < 0.01; * p-value < 0.05; ~ p-value < 0.10

Putting in Perspective the Learning Trajectories of Displaced Students

Our strategy to estimate the effects of school closings on displaced students is based on comparing the expected learning trajectory for displaced students with the actual one. Even though this is appropriate for isolating the effects due to school closings, it does not provide us with a reference to the magnitude of the estimated school closing effects. By looking at the differences in the achievement of the students who were attending the closing schools compared to similar students in other CPS schools, we can have a reference to judge the size of the school closing effects.

The achievement of students in closing schools was low compared to that of students with similar backgrounds who attended other CPS schools. Figure B shows the expected and actual reading achievement trajectories for displaced students who were 10 years old when their schools closed. The gray line is the achievement trajectory for similar students (in terms of gender, race/ethnicity, socioeconomic status, age, and special education status) who attend other CPS schools. Comparing the learning trajectory of displaced students to similar students enrolled in other schools, we find that by age eight displaced students were six months behind in reading.[34] This difference may be due to differences in the quality of their schools, but it also reflects differences in skills upon entering school. The annual growth in reading for displaced students is below what other CPS students experienced—putting them farther behind, by almost nine months, by the time they are 13 years old. The drop in learning experienced as a result of the announcement of the school closing is negligible compared to the achievement gap of students in closed schools to students in other schools.

FIGURE B

Learning trajectories for displaced students and similar students in other CPS schools

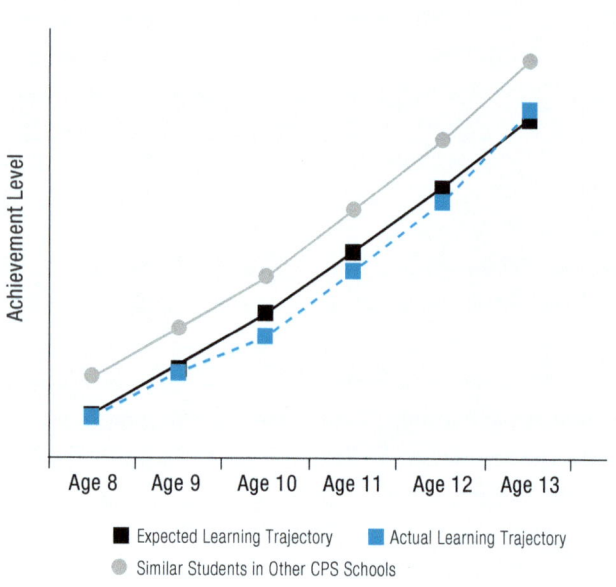

leaving the receiving schools with the task of providing summer school for displaced students in third, sixth, and eighth grade. However, a number of receiving schools reported having to wait several months before obtaining academic records for incoming displaced students—a delay which left some of these students without assignments for summer school that year.[35] The following summer, however, Summer Bridge enrollment rates for displaced students were similar to enrollment rates for students in the comparison group.

Students who changed schools because of school closings also had higher rates of subsequent school mobility (Figures 4 and 5). Prior to their schools' closing, displaced students had lower rates of school mobility during the school year than students in the comparison group. However, during their first year in a new school, they were twice as likely to change schools as the comparison group: nearly 11 percent of displaced students changed schools, while only 5 percent of students in the comparison group with similar characteristics did so (Figure 4). They were also more likely to change schools during the summer after their first year in a new school: 30 percent of the displaced students changed schools compared to only 14 percent

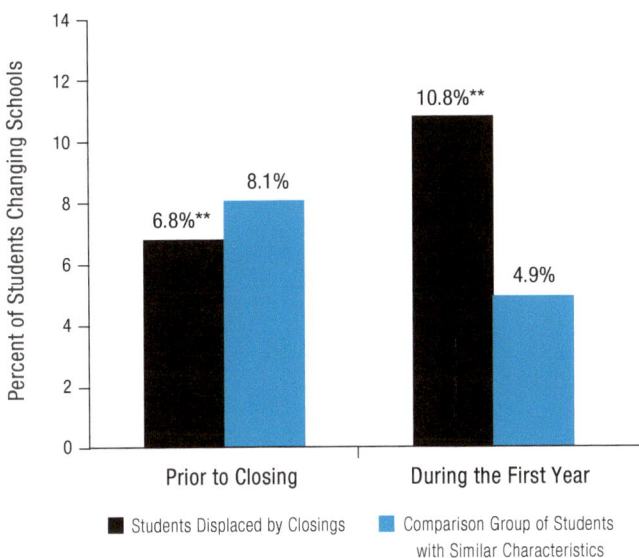

FIGURE 4

School closings made students more likely to change schools during the academic year (** p-value < 0.01)

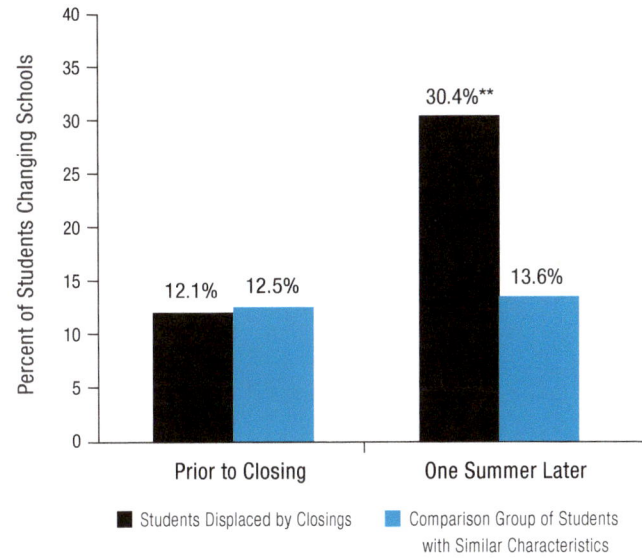

FIGURE 5

Displaced students were more likely to change schools over the summer

of students in the comparison group (Figure 5).[36]

Although our data do not indicate reasons for voluntary school moves, this finding suggests that a higher than expected proportion of displaced students did not find their receiving school to be a good fit. However, this higher rate of school mobility had no apparent impact on student achievement in subsequent years in new schools.

The school closing policy did not have an effect either on retention rates or on special education referrals for displaced students (Figures 6 and 7). Displaced students were no more or less likely than students in the comparison group to be retained in grade or to be referred to special education services before or after school closings. Even the fact that displaced students were less likely to attend Summer Bridge did not translate into higher retention rates. According to prior research on Summer Bridge, attendance in this program allowed low achieving students to raise their test scores, but students who were farthest behind were less likely to meet the promotion criteria.[37] Research also showed that students who attended Summer Bridge had smaller class sizes, as well as positive and supportive relationships with their teachers. Displaced students who did not attend Summer Bridge missed an opportunity to get to know some of their teachers and peers in the receiving schools before the start of the academic year.

Impact of School Closings on High School Outcomes

Given that the largest impact of school closings on achievement occurs during the announcement year, we ask whether students who were in eighth grade at the time their schools were closed were at a greater disadvantage than other students in lower grades when they moved to high school.[38] To answer this question, we look at the freshman on-track indicator, which provides an assessment of whether ninth-grade students are on-track to graduate within four years.[39]

Despite entering high school significantly behind in reading and in math, students whose schools closed at the end of their eighth-grade year were just as likely to be on-track at the end of their freshmen year as students in our comparison group. Displaced students in earlier grades who spent at least one year in elementary school after their schools closed entered high school with reading and math achievement at a level we would have expected had their schools not been closed. When we

Chapter 3 | 21

FIGURE 6
Displaced students were not retained in grade at higher rates in their receiving schools

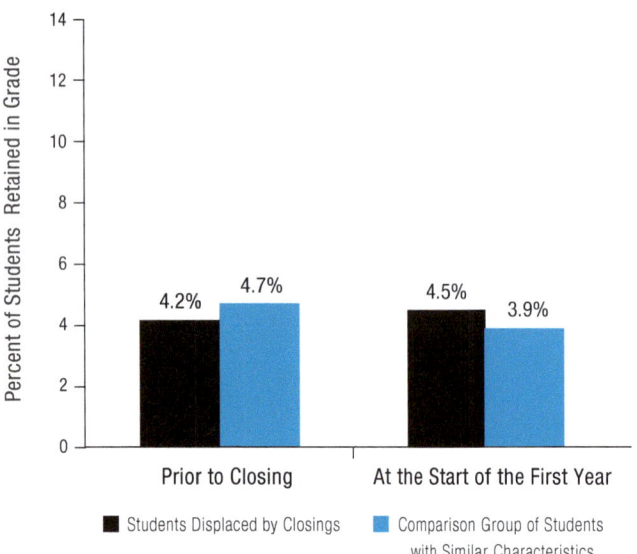

Note: ** p-value < 0.01; * p-value < 0.05; ~ p-value < 0.10

FIGURE 7
New referrals to special education services did not increase for displaced students

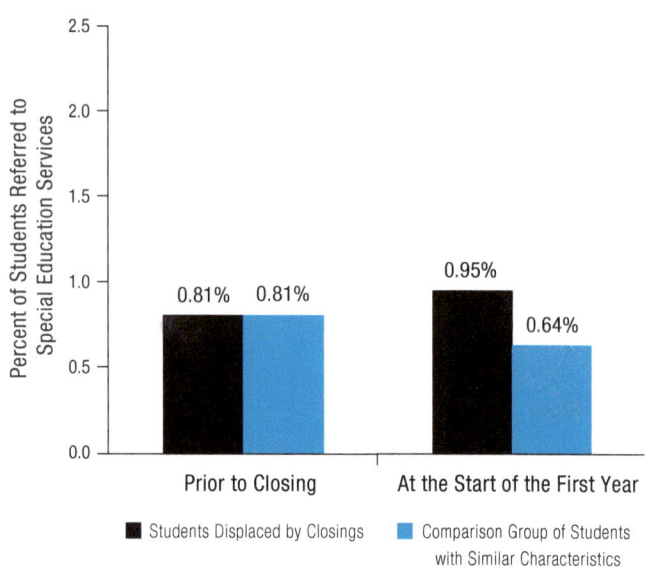

Note: ** p-value < 0.01; * p-value < 0.05; ~ p-value < 0.10

compared the likelihood of being on-track to graduate for these students to the comparison group of students, they were equally likely to be on-track at the end of their freshman year. The on-track to graduate rate was 48.1 percent for displaced students (see Figure 8).

Mitigating the Effect of School Closings on Achievement

Consistent with prior research on student mobility, characteristics of receiving schools had an effect on the learning of displaced students during their first year. Students who enrolled in schools with high average student achievement had significantly higher levels of achievement than students who enrolled in weaker schools. In reading, displaced students in the strongest receiving schools (those in the top quartile of the distribution) had an achievement level one year later that was almost a month above expected. However, students who attended some of the weakest schools in the system (those in the bottom quartile of the distribution) experienced a loss in achievement of over a month (see Figure 9). In math, the achievement level was more than two months above what was expected for students in the strongest schools, versus a loss of half a month for students in the weakest schools. The overall

FIGURE 8
School closings did not affect the percentage of students on-track to graduate at the end of their freshmen year

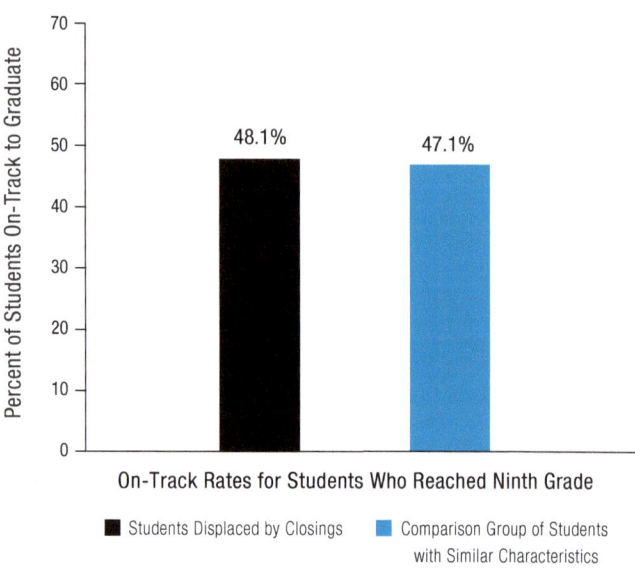

Note: ** p-value < 0.01; * p-value < 0.05; ~ p-value < 0.10

academic achievement of receiving schools affected math scores more than reading scores.

Displaced students who enrolled in receiving schools with high levels of positive interaction between students and teachers also showed higher learning gains (see sidebar for an explanation of how we

FIGURE 9

The higher the academic quality of the receiving school, the higher the achievement level of the displaced students during the first year; the effect is more pronounced for math than for reading

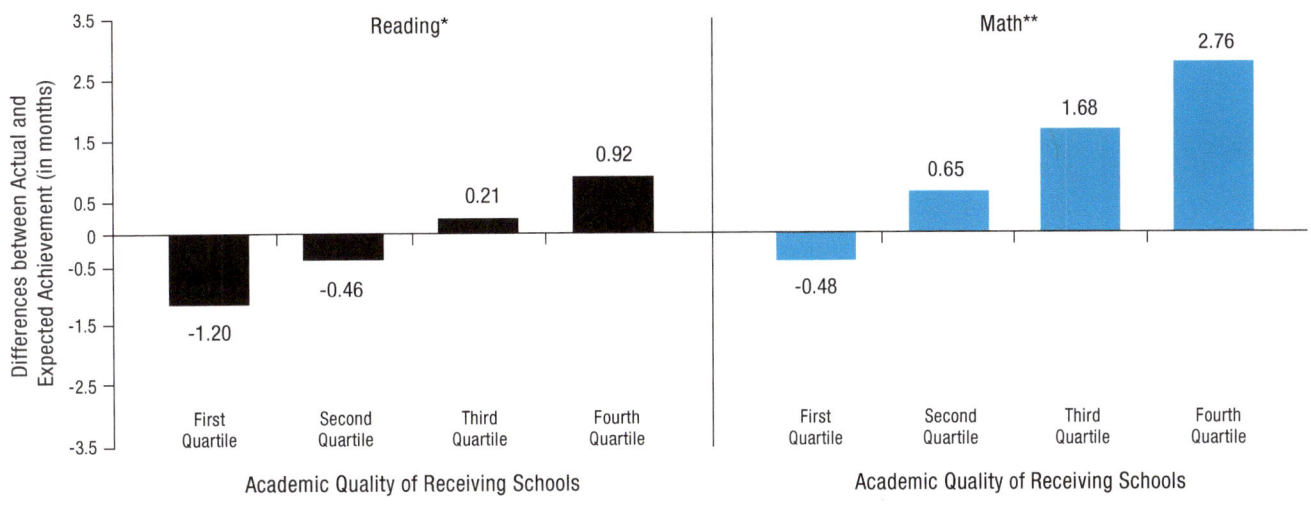

Note: ** p-value < 0.01; * p-value < 0.05; ~ p-value < 0.10

Measuring the Quality of Student-Teacher Interaction

Measures of the quality of student-teacher interaction come from surveys conducted by the Consortium on Chicago School Research (CCSR) every other year. CCSR gives surveys to students in sixth through twelfth grade, all teachers, and all principals. The particular measures on student-teacher interaction are created using students' responses.[40]

- **Teacher Personal Attention** measures the degree to which students perceive that their teachers give individual attention to their students and are concerned about them. Questions ask students if their teachers know and care about them, notice if they are having trouble in class, and are willing to help with academic and personal problems. High levels indicate that students frequently receive personalized support from their teachers.

- **Student-Teacher Trust** measures students' perceptions about the quality of their relationships with teachers. Questions ask students if teachers care about them, keep promises, listen to their ideas, and try to be fair. High levels indicate that there is trust and open communication between students and teachers.

measure interaction between students and teachers). For example, displaced students attending schools with low levels of teacher personal attention (bottom quartile) were two months behind their expected level (see Figure 10, Panel A). Among receiving schools, as the level of teacher personal attention increased, the difference between displaced students' expected and actual achievement is smaller. Displaced students who enrolled in receiving schools that were in the highest quartile for teacher personal attention learned somewhat more in reading than expected.[41] The effects on math are less pronounced, but they follow the same pattern.

Chapter 3 | 23

FIGURE 10

Teacher-student relationships matter in terms of making a positive transition; the effects are more pronounced for reading than for math

A. Teacher Personal Attention

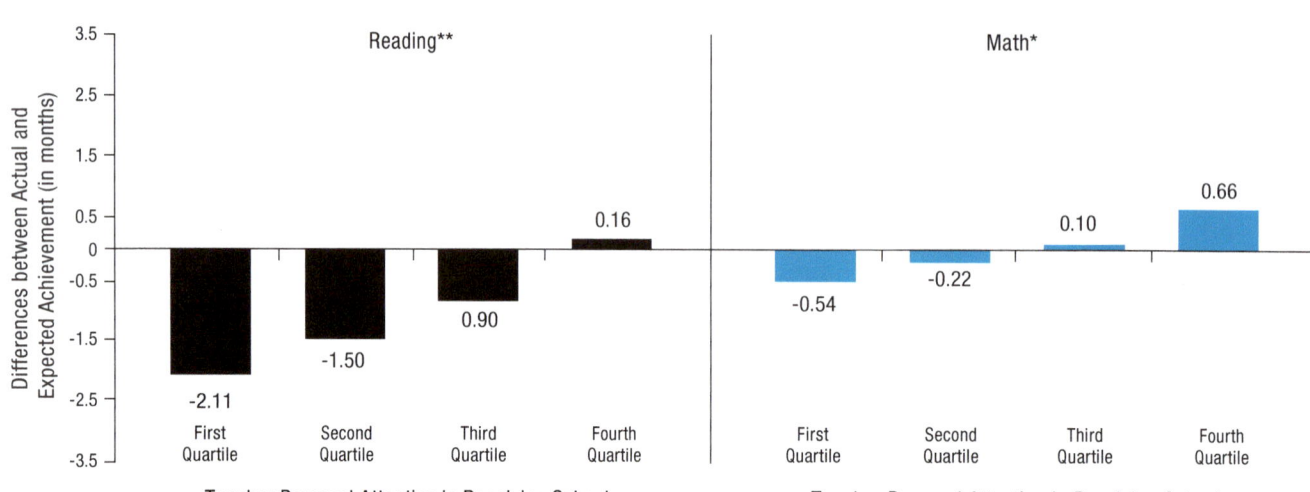

B. Student-Teacher Trust

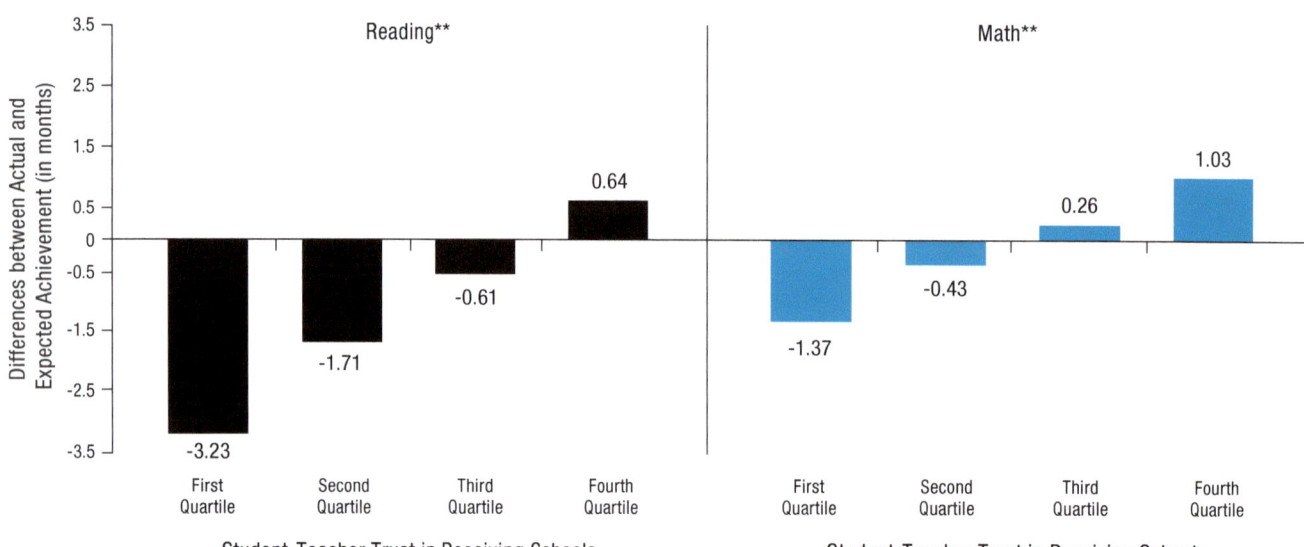

Note: ** p-value < 0.01; * p-value < 0.05; ~ p-value < 0.10

Similarly, students who enrolled in schools where there was a high level of trust between students and teachers had achievement levels of over half a month higher in reading and one month in math than expected. Students who were in schools with a low level of trust between students and teachers were more than three months behind their expected level in reading and more than a month behind in math.[42] Student-teacher interaction seemed to affect achievement in reading more than math.

We stressed here the importance of the relationships between students and teachers in explaining variations in students' achievement, but relationships among students could be equally important in terms of achievement. When these measures of peer interaction at the school level were included in the model, they did not correlate with differences in achievement among the displaced students.

Chapter 4

Interpretative Summary

Between 2001 and 2006, CPS closed 26 schools for underutilization or low performance. While nine were closed for poor academic performance and the rest for chronic underutilization, these distinctions were in name only in most cases. The majority of schools that were closed for poor performance also had very low enrollments, and most schools that were closed for underutilization also had very poor academic achievement. Understanding the effects of school closings on displaced students is important, given that CPS continues to implement this policy. Even though chronically low performing CPS schools are now being "turned around" instead of being closed, a large number of CPS schools are under-enrolled. There are calls for more closings of underutilized schools to save money.

As noted above, critics of the school closing policy have emphasized the disruption that changing schools may have on displaced students. While we did find that the announcement of a school closing has negative effects on students' achievement during the announcement year, achievement for these students returns to its predicted level after one year in their new school. Achievement for displaced students also remains at its expected trajectory two and three years later in both reading and math. In sum, the academic outlook for students did not change after their schools closed. Likewise, when displaced students reached high school, they were equally likely to be on-track to graduate as students in the comparison group.

> The success of a school closing policy crucially depends on a large supply of "better" schools and on an intentional strategy to enroll displaced students in these schools.

Although displaced students scored as expected during their first year in receiving schools, there was some variation in achievement growth based on the school these students attended. Displaced students who enrolled in top performing CPS schools had higher test scores one year later than displaced students who enrolled in low performing schools or in schools that were similar to the schools they left. This suggests that the academic outlook for displaced students would have been better had the receiving schools been dramatically better than the closing schools. However, only 6 percent of students enrolled in top performing CPS schools after they were displaced.

We also found that the differences between schools in the level of teacher support for students were critical in explaining variations in achievement for displaced students one year after the closings. Students who attended schools that had stronger student-teacher trust and teacher personal attention, as measured by CCSR's biennial survey, were more likely to make gains in reading and math. It is possible that displaced students who attended such schools had an easier transition into the new school and consequently were better able to learn.

Taken together, these findings suggest the theory behind the school closing policy has some merit. Students did better when they attended a better school after their schools closed. This also suggests that the success of a school closing policy crucially depends on a large supply of "better" schools and on an intentional strategy to enroll displaced students in these schools. Because most Chicago neighborhoods do not have stronger performing schools for displaced students to enter, parents must be willing and able to send their children to school away from their neighborhoods. This may explain why only 6 percent of students enrolled in top performing schools, and students who did enroll in top schools generally traveled longer distances to get to those schools.[43]

Two other findings are worth noting. The first is that displaced students were less likely to attend summer school when they were transitioning from the closing school to the receiving school. Schools closed at the end of the academic year, leaving receiving schools the task of providing summer school to students who needed it. Schools complained of not receiving information on incoming students in a timely matter, which might have prevented some students from attending summer school.

Another consequence of the policy was that displaced students were more likely to change schools in the future, both during the school academic year and during the summer. Part of the mobility we observed during the summer was related to new schools opening in the same building that had housed the closing school. However, even after taking this into account, displaced students were not only more mobile than they were before but also were more mobile than the students in the comparison group. Students who were forced to change schools because their schools were closed may have found it hard to fit into the new schools, thereby prompting a cycle of further school mobility.

In summary, we found few effects—either positive or negative—of school closings on the achievement of displaced students. Although reading and math gains were lower than expected once students found out their schools would soon close, these short-lived deficits were no longer evident after displaced students' first year in new schools. Changing schools neither resulted in additional negative effects on student achievement nor substantially improved the achievement of displaced students. Only the small number of students who transferred to academically strong receiving schools and found supportive teachers at these schools made significant gains in their learning.

References

Allensworth, Elaine M., and John Q. Easton (2005)
The on-track indicator as a predictor of high school graduation. Chicago: Consortium on Chicago School Research.

Anderson, Veronica (2006)
Slow progress amid ongoing strife over closings and displaced kids. *Catalyst.* March 2006.

Caputo, Angela (2009)
The case of the missing school closings report. Available at http://www.progressillinois.com/2009/3/30/missing-school-closings-report.

CBS (2009)
Board votes unanimously to close 16 city schools. Available at http://cbs2chicago.com/local/chicago.schools.closing.2.943969.html.

Chicago Public Schools (2008)
CPS FY2009 Budget Book. Available at http://www.cps.edu/About_CPS/Financial_information/Documents/FY09_Budget_Book_Online.pdf.

Chicago Public Schools (2009)
CPS moves to turn around six more schools. Available at http://www.cps.edu/News/Press_releases/2009/Pages/01_16_2009_PR1.aspx.

Duffrin, Elizabeth (2006)
Displaced kids "doing poorly." *Catalyst.* March 2006.

Goerge, Robert, John Dilts, Duck-Hye Yang, Miriam Wasserman, and Anne Clary (2007)
Chicago children and youth 1990–2010: Changing population trends and their implications for services. Chicago: Chapin Hall Center for Children at the University of Chicago.

Hanushek, Eric A., John F. Kain, and Steven G. Rivkin (2004)
Disruption versus tiebout improvement: The costs and benefits of switching schools, *Journal of Public Economics,* 88/9–10: 1,721–46.

Lipman, Pauline, and Alecia S. Person (2007)
Students as collateral damage? A preliminary study of Renaissance 2010 school closings in the Mid-South. Unpublished manuscript.

Neighborhood Capital Budget Group
Underutilization. Available at http://www.ncbg.org/schools/underutilization.htm.

Pribesh, Shana, and Douglas B. Downey (1999)
Why are residential and school moves associated with poor school performance? *Demography,* 36(4): 521–34.

Roderick, Melissa, Mimi Engel, and Jenny Nagaoka (2003)
Ending Social Promotion in Chicago: Results from Summer Bridge. Chicago: Consortium on Chicago School Research.

Rumberger, Russell (2003)
The causes and consequences of student mobility. *Journal of Negro Education,* 72(1): 6–21.

Rumberger, Russell, Katherine A. Larson, Robert K. Ream, and Gregory J. Palardy (1999)
The educational consequences of mobility for California students and schools. Berkeley, CA: Policy Analysis for California Education.

Sadovi, Carlos (2007)
Duncan: 50 schools could close. *Chicago Tribune,* December 20.

Appendix A:
School Closings and New Openings

Appendix A contains the list of schools that closed between 2001 and 2006 and the reason for their closings. It also includes information on whether a new school opened in same building. In addition, we report the year the new school opened, the grades it served, and the type of school.

TABLE 4

Last Year in Operation	Closing School Name	Reason for Closing	New School Opened	First Year in Operation	Grades Served First Year (at full capacity)	Type of School
2000–01	Riis	Underutilization	—			
	Near North	Condition of the Building	—			
2001–02	Dodge	Academic Reasons	Dodge Renaissance Academy	2003–04	K-8 (K-8)	Prof. Develop. School[44]
	Williams	Academic Reasons	Williams Multiplex	2003–04	K-3 (K-5)	Prof. Develop. School
			Williams Prep. Academy	2003–04	4-8 (6-8)	Traditional School
			KIPP Chicago Youth Village Academy[45]	2003–04	4-5 (5-7)	Contract School[46]
			Big Picture HS at Williams[47]	2003–04	9 (9-12)	Small School–CHSRI[48]
	Terrell	Academic Reasons	ACE Technical	2004–05	9 (9-12)	Charter School[49]
2002–03	Colman	Underutilization	—			
	Donoghue	Underutilization	U of C Charter – Donoghue	2005–06	PK, K-3 (PK, K-5)	Charter School
	Woodson North Middle	Underutilization	U of C Charter – Woodson	2008–09	6-8 (6-8)	Charter School
	Arts of Living	Underutilization	—			
	Tesla	Underutilization	—			
	Flower Career Academy	Change in Educational Focus	Al Raby	2004–05	9 (9-12)	Small School–CHSRI
	Muñoz Marin	Other	—			
	Recovering the Gifted Child	Unknown	—			
2003–04	Byrd	Underutilization	—			
	Douglas	Underutilization	Pershing West Middle	2005–06	4-8 (4-8)	Performance School[50]

TABLE 4 CONTINUED

Last Year in Operation	Closing School Name	Reason for Closing	New School Opened	First Year in Operation	Grades Served First Year (at full capacity)	Type of School
2003–04	Hartigan	Underutilization	Bronzeville Lighthouse	2006–07	K-5 (PK, K-8)	Charter School
	Jefferson	Underutilization	—			
	Raymond	Underutilization	Perspectives Charter IIT Math and Science Academy	2008–09	6, 7, 9 (6-12)	Charter School
	Suder	Underutilization	Suder Montessori	2005–06	PK, K (PK, K-8)	Performance School
	Doolittle West	Underutilization	—			
	Truth	Underutilization	—			
	Spaulding Elem.	Underutilization	—			
	Spaulding High	Underutilization	—			
	Wright	Condition of the Building	—			
	Orr	Change in Educational Focus	Phoenix Military Academy[51]	2002–03	9-12 (9-12)	Small School – CHSRI
			Mose Vines	2003–04	9-12 (9-12)	Small School – CHSRI
			AASTA	2004–05	9-12 (9-12)	Small School – CHSRI
			EXCEL[52]	2004–05	9-12 (9-12)	Small School – CHSRI
2004–05	Grant	Academic Reasons	Marine Military Academy	2007–08	9 (9-12)	Performance School
	Howland	Academic Reasons	Catalyst Charter Howland	2006–07	4-5 (K-8)	Charter School
	Bunche	Academic Reasons	Providence Englewood Charter	2006–07	K-5 (K-8)	Charter School
	South Shore	Change in Educational Focus	School of the Arts	2002–03	9, 11 (9-12)	Small School – CHSRI
			School of Entrepreneurship	2002–03	9-10 (9-12)	Small School – CHSRI
			School of Technology	2003–04	9 (9-12)	Small School – CHSRI
			School of Leadership	2003–04	9-12 (9-12)	Small School – CHSRI
	Anderson	Unknown	—			

TABLE 4 CONTINUED

Last Year in Operation	Closing School Name	Reason for Closing	New School Opened	First Year in Operation	Grades Served First Year (at full capacity)	Type of School
2005–06	Arai	Underutilization	UPLIFT Community School	2005–06	6-9 (6-12)	Performance School
	Lindblom	Condition of the Building	Lindblom Math and Science	2005–06	9 (7-12)	Performance School
	DuSable	Alternative Use of the School	Dale Hale Williams	2005–06	7 (7-12)	Performance School
			DuSable Leadership Academy	2005–06	9 (9-12)	Charter School
			Bronzeville Scholastic	2005–06	9 (9-12)	Performance School
	Bowen	Alternative Use of the School	BEST	2002–03	9 (9-12)	Small School – CHSRI
			Chicago Discovery Academy	2002–03	9-12 (9-12)	Small School – CHSRI
			Global Visions	2003–04	9 (9-12)	Small School – CHSRI
			New Millennium	2004–05	9 (9-12)	Small School – CHSRI
	KIPP	Alternative Use of the School	—			
	Farren	Academic Reasons	—			
	Morse	Academic Reasons	Polaris Charter Academy	2007–08	K-2 (K-8)	Charter School
	Frazier	Academic Reasons	Frazier International Magnet	2007–08	K-5 (K-8)	Performance School
			Frazier Prep. Academy	2007–08	K-5 (K-8)	Contract School

Appendix A

Appendix B:
Data, Analytic Methods, and Variables Used

Data

The data for this study come from CPS student administrative data detailing enrollment information, test scores, and high school transcript information for students enrolled in CPS. These data have been collected since the early 1990s. The data on student achievement are based on the Iowa Tests of Basic Skills (ITBS), which students from third through eighth grade had been required to take every spring. CPS stopped administering this test after the spring of 2005.

Three additional sources of data were employed for school level information. The first comes from the annual State Report Cards. This report card is created for each school and includes such school level indicators as attendance. Data on design capacity for each school come from the Department of School Demographics and Planning at CPS. We also rely on survey data collected biannually by the Consortium on Chicago School Research. The survey is administered to students in sixth through twelfth grade, all teachers, and all principals. The responses to the surveys allow us to gauge different areas of schools' climate.

Analytic Methods

The decision to close a school is not random; rather, it is based on different school indicators. In order to assess the effects of school closings on students, we exploit the fact that we have several observations for students prior to the intervention and several observations after the intervention. For example, we can use longitudinal data to estimate the learning trajectory of students in reading and math and determine whether the learning trajectory deviates from the expected one after the intervention. If there are other factors that affect the displaced students and that occur at the same time as the school closings, the estimated effects might be the combination of both occurrences. To strengthen our research design, we incorporate a comparison group of students for whom we have data as well longitudinal data on different outcomes. If we can show that this comparison group is equivalent to the students affected by school closings prior to the closing, then the differences observed after closings are likely attributable to the school closings.

Since our research question focuses on what would have happened to displaced students had their schools remained open, the comparison group of students is based on students attending similar schools because their learning trajectories, in the absence of school closings, should be similar. We use propensity score matching and select schools that look similar to closing schools based on the variables related to capacity utilization and performance of the school. The variables are listed in Table 5.

We picked matching schools from the estimation of two different models. One estimated the probability of closing for low performance. This model only used schools that were on probation. The second model estimated the probability of closing for low enrollment. This model only included schools that had 65 percent or lower capacity utilization. Decisions on closing schools are made in the middle of an academic year. Therefore, CPS leaders make decisions with data available at that point, which is the data from the previous year. For example, decisions made in 2005–06 were based on data from the academic year 2004–05. For that reason, the probability of being closed on a particular year is modeled as a function of variables from the prior year.

For each closed school, we selected a matching school with a similar probability of closing and similar student racial composition as well as grade structure. We picked one matching school for each closing school. Table 5 contains information on school level indicators for the closing schools and the matching schools for the year before closing. Table 5 shows that closing schools and matching schools are very similar in all of the indicators.

The 18 closing schools in our sample enrolled 5,445 students just before they closed. There were 6,534 students enrolled in the matching schools. To study the effects of school closings on achievement and other outcomes, we restrict our sample to students eight years and older since they are supposed to take the annual ITBS test. Of the students enrolled in the closing schools, 3,777 students were in that group compared to 4,683 students in the matching schools.

TABLE 5

School indicators for the year prior to closing and differences with matching schools

	Closed Schools	Matching Schools	Difference with Comparison Group (p-values)
Percent Capacity Utilization	32.9%	36.8%	3.9% (0.32)
Percent Students from Attendance Area	48.3%	48.5%	0.2% (0.98)
Percent of Students at or above Norms in ITBS Reading	20.8%	21.1%	0.3% (0.88)
4-year Average Percent of Students at or above Norms in ITBS Reading	21.0%	22.1%	1.1% (0.50)
Percent of Students Meeting or Exceeding Standards ISAT Composite	21.0%	22.9%	1.9% (0.34)
4-year Average Percent of Students Meeting or Exceeding Standards ISAT Composite	19.9%	22.0%	2.1% (0.24)
Average Annual Student Gain in ITBS Reading	0.78	0.80	0.02 (0.76)
4-year Average Annual Student Gain in ITBS Reading	0.95	0.93	-0.02 (0.68)
Percent of Students Making Negative Gains in ITBS Reading	29.8%	29.9%	0.1% (0.97)
Mobility Rate	35.9%	34.5%	-1.4% (0.72)
Attendance Rate	91.0%	91.2%	0.2% (0.64)
Truancy Rate	4.9%	9.1%	4.2% (0.12)
Percent Low Income	96.5%	95.1%	-1.4% (0.45)

Note: Significant differences would have p-values less than 0.05

Analysis of Achievement Data

We estimate the learning trajectories for reading and math using a three-level hierarchical model: the first level is a measurement model that adjusts for the reliability of the standardized test scores, the second level is repeated observations for students, and the third level represents students. Our achievement measure is based on Rasch scores from the ITBS data.[53] In particular, the model is:

Level 1

$$\frac{\text{Achievement}_{jk}}{s_{jk}} = \pi_{jk} \frac{1}{s_{jk}} + e_{jk},$$

where $e_{jk} \sim N(0,1)$, s_{jk}, is the standard error estimated from the Rasch analysis for student k at age j and π_{jk} is the student's true ability at age j, adjusted for measurement error.

Level 2

$$\pi_{jk} = \beta_{0k} + \beta_{1k}(\text{Age})_{jk} + \beta_{2k}(\text{Age Squared})_{jk} + \beta_{3k}(\text{Year Announcement Closing})_{jk} + \beta_{4k}(\text{Year One After Closing})_{jk} + \beta_{5k}(\text{Year Two After Closing})_{jk} + \beta_{6k}(\text{Year Three After Closing})_{jk} + r_{jk}$$

The true ability of the student is modeled as a function of age and age squared to allow for non-linear learning trajectories. Age takes a value of 0 when the age is eight, 1 when the age is nine, and so on. Therefore, the intercept represents the true ability of the student at age eight. The other variables are dummy variables that indicate the timing of the announcement of a closing, the year after a closing, and two and three years later for students affected by a closing. The estimates for these variables represent deviations from the learning trajectory of displaced students in the year the closing was announced and the year after the school closed.

Since the first closing in our sample is at the end of the academic year 2000–01 and ITBS was administered last in the spring of 2005, we have enough observations to estimate only up to three years of effects. Effects after two and three years are estimated by limiting the sample to students to those with three years worth of data after closing. These long-run effect estimates are based mainly on displaced students whose schools closed towards the beginning of our sample. Only students whose schools closed in 2000–01 and 2001–02 and who were in fifth grade or lower have enough data points for the three-year mark. Also, students affected by closings in 2005 and 2006 helped with the estimation of the learning trajectory pre-closing but not post-closing.

Level 3

$$\beta_{0k} = \gamma_{00} + \gamma_{01}(\text{Cohort 97})_k + \ldots + \gamma_{09}(\text{Cohort 05})_k + \gamma_{010}(\text{Age 9 Risk Closing})_k + \ldots + \gamma_{015}(\text{Age more 13 Risk Closing})_k + \gamma_{016}(\text{Social Status})_k + \gamma_{017}(\text{Concentration Poverty})_k + \gamma_{018}(\text{Female})_k + \gamma_{019}(\text{Special Education at Age 8})_k + \gamma_{020}(\text{Closing})_k + u_{0k}$$

$$\beta_{1k} = \gamma_{10} + \gamma_{11}(\text{Cohort 97})_k + \ldots + \gamma_{17}(\text{Cohort 03})_k + \gamma_{18}(\text{Age 9 Risk Closing})_k + \ldots + \gamma_{113}(\text{Age more 13 Risk Closing})_k + \gamma_{114}(\text{Social Status})_k + \gamma_{115}(\text{Concentration Poverty})_k + \gamma_{116}(\text{Female})_k + \gamma_{117}(\text{Special Education at Age 8})_k + \gamma_{118}(\text{Special Education at Age 8})_k + u_{1k}$$

$$\beta_{2k} = \gamma_{20} + u_{2k}$$

$$\beta_{nk} = \gamma_{n0} \text{ for the rest of the variables.}$$

The initial ability at age eight and the growth are modeled as a function of the cohort and other characteristics of the students (e.g., gender, social status, poverty) and whether students were receiving special education services at the age of eight. The intercept, slope, and curvature in the model are allowed to vary by student as indicated by the random components. This allows us to estimate a different growth trajectory for each student.

We also include a few dummy variables to indicate the age at which students faced the risk of closings. Students are compared to other students who face the risk of closings at the same age (a description of all these variables can be found after the description of the analytical models). In modeling the intercept, we include a dummy variable indicating which students were affected by closings to test whether the comparison group of students is similar to the group of displaced students. These estimates are not statistically different from zero in our models, showing that the comparison group of students was similar to the students affected by school closings in the years prior to the closing.

In addition, we estimated different variations of the model by including time varying variables such as retention. The estimates of the school closing effects were very consistent in each of our model variations.

To investigate whether there was variation in students' achievement a year after they moved from their closing schools based on characteristics of the receiving schools, the Level 3 equation for the coefficient representing the effect of one year after the closing was modified as follows: $\beta_{4k} = \gamma_{40} + \gamma_{41}$ (School Characteristic), allowing the effect year one after the closing to be a function of different school characteristics.

Analysis of Other Outcomes

We also were interested in studying the effects of school closings on such outcomes as attendance to summer school, retention, referral to special education services, and mobility. The explanatory variables in these models were a set of student characteristics (e.g., gender, SES, whether students are old for their grade, dummies for the cohort, age at risk of facing closings) and a series of dummies for years prior to closings and years after closings. There are several observations in these analyses for each student. However, there is not enough variation at the student level to take into account the clustering of the data. Since all of these outcomes are variables that take values of 0 or 1, the models were estimated using a logistic model.

The last outcome we studied was a measure of high school performance. Although most students had not reached the point where we could see whether they graduated, a good number of them reached high school. Therefore, we compared the on-track to graduate indicator in the freshmen year for displaced students and students who attended schools that were similar to those that were closing. For this analysis, we only had one observation per student so we cannot compare how students did before and after the closing. Therefore, we rely only on the comparison of the displaced students to the comparison group.

Description of the Variables Used in the Analyses

Age	Based on the students' birth date, we calculate the age of the student on September 1 each year. We then rescale it to 0 for students whose age is eight years old, 1 for nine years old, etc.
Year that the Closing Was Announced	Coded 1 for observations during the announcement year and only for students affected by school closings; 0 otherwise.
Year One after the Closing	Coded 1 for observations one year after the closing took place and only for students affected by school closings; 0 otherwise.
Year Two after the Closing	Coded 1 for observations two years after the closing took place and only for students affected by school closings; 0 otherwise.
Year Three after the Closing	Coded 1 for observations three years after the closing took place and only for students affected by school closings; 0 otherwise.
Cohort97—Cohort05	These are a series of dummy variables reflecting the cohorts of third-grade students in the analyses. For example, *cohort97* is coded as 1 if a student was in third grade in the academic year 1996–97; 0 otherwise.
Age 9 Risk Closing— Age More 13 Risk Closing	These are a series of dummy variables reflecting the age of the students when they face the possibility of a closing. For example, age 9 risk closing is coded as 1 if a student was nine years old when he/she faced his/her school closing, or for students in the comparison group when their school was in similar circumstances even though the school was not closed; 0 otherwise.
Social Status	This variable is based on 2000 U.S. Census data on the block group in which students live. It contains two indicators: the log of the percentage of employed persons 16 years old or older who are managers or executives and the mean level of education among people 18 years old or older.
Concentration of Poverty	This variable is based on 2000 U.S. Census data on the block group in which students live. It contains two reverse-coded indicators: the log of the percentage of male residents over age 18 employed one or more weeks during the year and the log of the percentage of families above the poverty line.
Gender	Coded 1 for female students; 0 for male students.
Special Education	Coded 1 for students who are receiving special education services; 0 otherwise.
Closing	Coded 1 for students affected by school closings; 0 otherwise.
School Characteristics	There were several school characteristics that we explored in our analyses. They were: **School Average Achievement Level.** We calculated the percent of students at or above norms on ITBS reading and then assigned a percentile to each school based on the distribution of CPS schools. **Teacher Personal Attention.** It measures the degree to which students perceive that their teachers give individual attention to and are concerned about their students. Students were asked the extent to which they would agree (strongly disagree to strongly agree) that their teacher: (1) notices if I have trouble learning something; (2) really listens to what I have to say; (3) believes I can do well in school; (4) is willing to give extra help on schoolwork if I need it; and (5) helps me catch up if am behind. The measure is constructed using Rasch rating scale analysis and represents the average of students' reports in the school. For our analysis, the school averages are standardized to have mean 0 and standard deviation equal to 1. **Student-Teacher Trust.** It measures students' perceptions about the quality of their relationships with teachers. Students were asked the extent to which they would agree (strongly disagree to strongly agree) that: (1) my teachers really care about me; (2) my teachers always keep their promises; (3) my teachers always try to be fair; (4) I feel safe and comfortable with my teacher at this school; (5) when my teacher tells me not to do something, I know he/she has a good reason; and (6) my teachers treat me with respect. The measure is constructed using Rasch rating scale analysis and represents the average of students' reports in the school. For our analysis, the school averages are standardized to have mean 0 and standard deviation equal to 1.

Endnotes

Executive Summary

1 Chicago Public Schools (January 16, 2009).
2 Chicago Public Schools (January 16, 2009).
3 We limit the sample to schools closed between 2001 and 2006 due to a change in the standardized tests in 2006.
4 Summer Bridge is a mandatory summer program for students in third, sixth, and eighth grades who do not meet the promotion criteria in the spring. Students who are successful at the end of the program are promoted to the next grade, while the rest are retained.
5 Measures of the quality of student-teacher interaction come from surveys conducted by CCSR every other year. Questions measure the degree to which students perceive that their teachers give them individual attention and measure students' perceptions of the quality of their relationships with their teachers.

Introduction

6 CPS budget documents state that some of the savings come from closings schools that were under-enrolled (Chicago Public Schools, 2008).
7 Rumberger (2003).
8 Pribesh and Downy (1999).
9 Rumberger et al. (1999).
10 Lipman and Person (2007).
11 Hanushek, Kain, and Rivkin (2004).

Chapter 1

12 Visit http://policy.cps.k12.il.us/documents/410.4.pdf for the full policy document on school closings.
13 Goerge et al. (2007).
14 In 2000 the CHA launched its Plan for Transformation, which called for the demolition and redevelopment of many of its public housing projects and the rehabilitation of other public housing units. Although public housing buildings had been demolished in the past, the plan's scale was much larger.
15 Visit the website of the Neighborhood Capital Budget Group and click on "Underutilization."
16 It is possible that because neighborhoods had fewer school-aged children and because the schools' enrollment started to decline, these schools were receiving students from overcrowded schools.
17 Sadovi (2007).
18 CBS (2009).
19 Caputo (2009).
20 The open enrollment policy establishes that students can submit applications to any CPS neighborhood school with open seats. In addition, students can apply to magnet and charter schools.
21 Duffrin (2006).
22 In 2006, CPS specified new supports to help receiving schools and displaced students during the transition period. See Duffrin (2006).

Chapter 2

23 Duffrin (2006).
24 Hanushek, Kain, and Rivkin (2004).
25 Of the 13 elementary schools closed for underutilization, two were consolidated with nearby schools: Woodson North was consolidated with Woodson South, and Doolittle West was consolidated with Doolittle Middle. In these two cases, nearly all the teachers and students from the closing school transferred to the nearby consolidated school. Because these students transferred with all their teachers and classmates, their experience is likely to be very different from what other students experienced when their schools were closed. As a result, they are not included in this study.

Another school, Truth, only served primary grades; since standardized testing starts in third grade, we do not have information on these students' achievement prior to their school closing. As a result, these students are not included in the study.

Finally, Arai was a middle school that was phased out grade-by-grade, which eliminated the need for these students to transfer out. Therefore, these students are not part of this study.
26 The announcement of school closings might have increased the rate at which students left the schools before the end of the academic year. Our data do not allow us to determine either when exactly a student leaves school (whether it is before or after the announcement) or whether the move was due to the school closing.
27 The Department of School Demographics and Planning at CPS provided the capacity numbers for each school. We calculated the percent capacity utilization by dividing the number of students enrolled in schools by the capacity of the school.
28 Of the 5,445 students enrolled in these 18 schools, 110 were affected by elementary school closings two times.
29 Our data allow us to calculate the distance from the residences of the students to their schools. This distance is calculated as a straight line from one point (the home address of the student) to another (the address of the school).

Chapter 3

30 Anderson (2006).

31 Displaced students' reading achievement was about three-quarters of a month behind the expected level; however, this difference is not statistically significant using the standard criteria for evaluating significance.

32 The long-term effects are estimated only with data from students for whom we had three years worth of data after school closings. Students with three years worth of data are those affected by closings in early grades and also those affected by the early school closings since ITBS was administered last in the spring of 2005. The one-year effect is estimated with all students eight years and older.

33 Although the effect on reading achievement is similar in size to the one that students experienced during the announcement year, the smaller sample that we use to estimate long-term effects of school closings limits our ability to conclude that the effect is statistically significant.

34 We do not imply that all the differences we see between displaced students' achievement and similar students' achievement are due to the schools they attended. Even though we matched students based on all the student characteristics we had available to us, we did not match them based on their ability. Much of the differences might be due to differences in ability prior to entering school.

35 Duffrin (2006).

36 Some students changed schools to attend schools that had reopened in the buildings formerly occupied by a school that had been closed. But differences in student mobility remained significant, even after taking this into account.

37 Roderick, Engel, and Nagaoka (2003).

38 This analysis is based on students who had reached ninth grade by the fall of 2007 or earlier. Twenty-five percent of the displaced students were still in elementary schools in 2007, while 63 percent had reached ninth grade.

39 Students who are on-track to graduate receive at least five course credits and no more than one F during their freshmen year, and they are four times more likely to graduate in four years than students who are off-track to graduate. See Allensworth and Easton (2005).

40 Visit http://ccsr.uchicago.edu/content/page.php?cat=4 for more information about CCSR surveys.

41 Almost 40 percent of displaced students attended receiving schools with high levels of teacher personal attention, with 15 percent of students attending schools with low levels of teacher personal attention.

42 Only 2 percent of displaced students attended receiving schools with low levels of student-teacher trust. Twenty percent of the displaced students attended the strongest schools in terms of student-teacher trust.

Interpretative Summary

43 In 2007, CPS modified the school closing policy so that schools could not be closed if there were no higher performing schools nearby.

Appendix A

44 A professional development school is a site for the training of future teachers.

45 Closed at the end of 2005–06.

46 Contract schools are schools operated by an independent non-profit organization. These schools have an advisory body comprised of staff, parents, and community members.

47 Closed at the end of 2006–07.

48 Small school-CHSRI is a high school created as part of the Chicago High School Redesign Initiative, which aimed to open close to two dozen small high schools in Chicago.

49 Charter schools are public schools operated by independent non-profit organizations. They are not subject to the same policies and laws as traditional public schools.

50 Performance schools are schools operated by CPS. Their staff is part of CPS, and they have a Local School Council. They have more flexibility in their curriculum, school schedule, and budget than traditional CPS schools.

51 After a move to another location at the end of the 2004–05 academic year, this school was no longer part of CHSRI.

52 The three remaining schools were closed at the end of 2007–08. A new school (Orr Academy High School) opened in the fall of 2008. Orr Academy is a performance school.

Appendix B

53 CCSR converted ITBS scores into a logit metric using Rasch models. Rasch scores can be compared easily across time, different test forms, and levels. Because the metric is not easily interpretable, we translated all our results into months of learning.

About the Authors

Marisa de la Torre

Marisa de la Torre is a Senior Research Analyst at the Consortium on Chicago School Research. Before joining the Consortium, she worked for the Chicago Public Schools at the Office of Research, Evaluation, and Accountability. Her previous research focused on the Chicago High School Redesign Initiative and student mobility. She received a master's degree in economics from Northwestern University.

Julia Gwynne

Julia Gwynne is a Senior Research Analyst at the Consortium on Chicago School Research. Her research interests include student mobility, curriculum policies, and special education. She received a PhD in sociology from the University of Chicago.

This report reflects the interpretation of the authors. Although the CCSR's Steering Committee provided technical advice and reviewed earlier versions, no formal endorsement by these individuals or organizations, should be assumed.

This report was produced by the Consortium's publications and communications staff: Claire Durwood; Chris Mazzeo, associate director for policy and outreach; and Emily Krone, senior manager for outreach and publications.

Editing by Ann Lindner
Graphic Design by Jeff Hall Design
Photos by Carey Primeau, David Schalliol, and David N. Marque

10-09/1M/jhdesign

Consortium on Chicago School Research

Directors

Penny Bender Sebring
Interim Co-Executive Director
Founding Co-Director
Consortium on Chicago
School Research

Elaine M. Allensworth
Interim Co-Executive Director
Consortium on Chicago
School Research

Melissa Roderick
Hermon Dunlap Smith Professor
School of Social Service
Administration
University of Chicago

Steering Committee

Arie J. van der Ploeg, *Co-Chair*
Learning Point Associates

Steve Zemelman, *Co-Chair*
Illinois Network of
Charter Schools

Institutional Members

Barbara J. Eason-Watkins
Chicago Public Schools

Steve L. Washington
Chicago Board of Education

Marilyn Stewart
Chicago Teachers Union

Individual Members

Veronica Anderson
Stanford University

Carolyn Epps
Chicago Public Schools

Cornelia Grumman
Ounce of Prevention

Timothy Knowles
Urban Education Institute

Janet Knupp
Chicago Public
Education Fund

Sarah Kremsner
Chicago Public Schools

Dennis Lacewell
Urban Prep Charter Academy
for Young Men

Lila Leff
Umoja Student Development
Corporation

Peter Martinez
University of Illinois
at Chicago

Ruanda Garth McCullough
Loyola University

Gregory Michie
Illinois State University

Brian Spittle
DePaul University

Matthew Stagner
Chapin Hall Center
for Children

Amy Treadwell
Chicago New Teacher Center

Josie Yanguas
Illinois Resource Center

Kim Zalent
Business and Professional
People for the Public Interest

Martha Zurita
Youth Connection
Charter School

Our Mission

The Consortium on Chicago School Research (CCSR) at the University of Chicago Urban Education Institute conducts research of high technical quality that can inform and assess policy and practice in the Chicago Public Schools. We seek to expand communication among researchers, policy makers, and practitioners as we support the search for solutions to the problems of school reform. CCSR encourages the use of research in policy action and improvement of practice, but does not argue for particular policies or programs. Rather, we help to build capacity for school reform by identifying what matters for student success and school improvement, creating critical indicators to chart progress, and conducting theory-driven evaluation to identify how programs and policies are working.

www.ingramcontent.com/pod-product-compliance
Lightning Source LLC
Chambersburg PA
CBHW060822090426
42738CB00002B/77